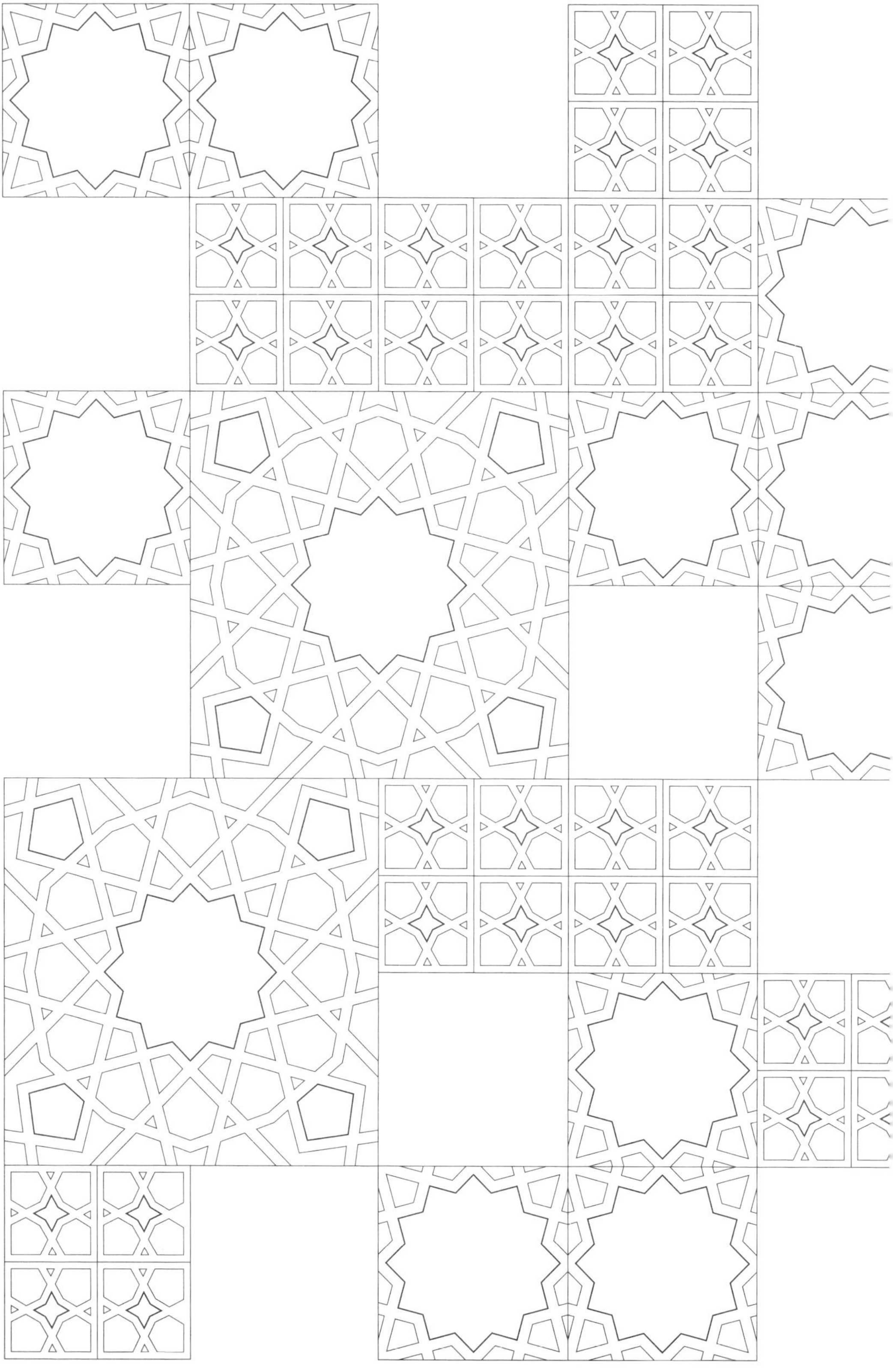

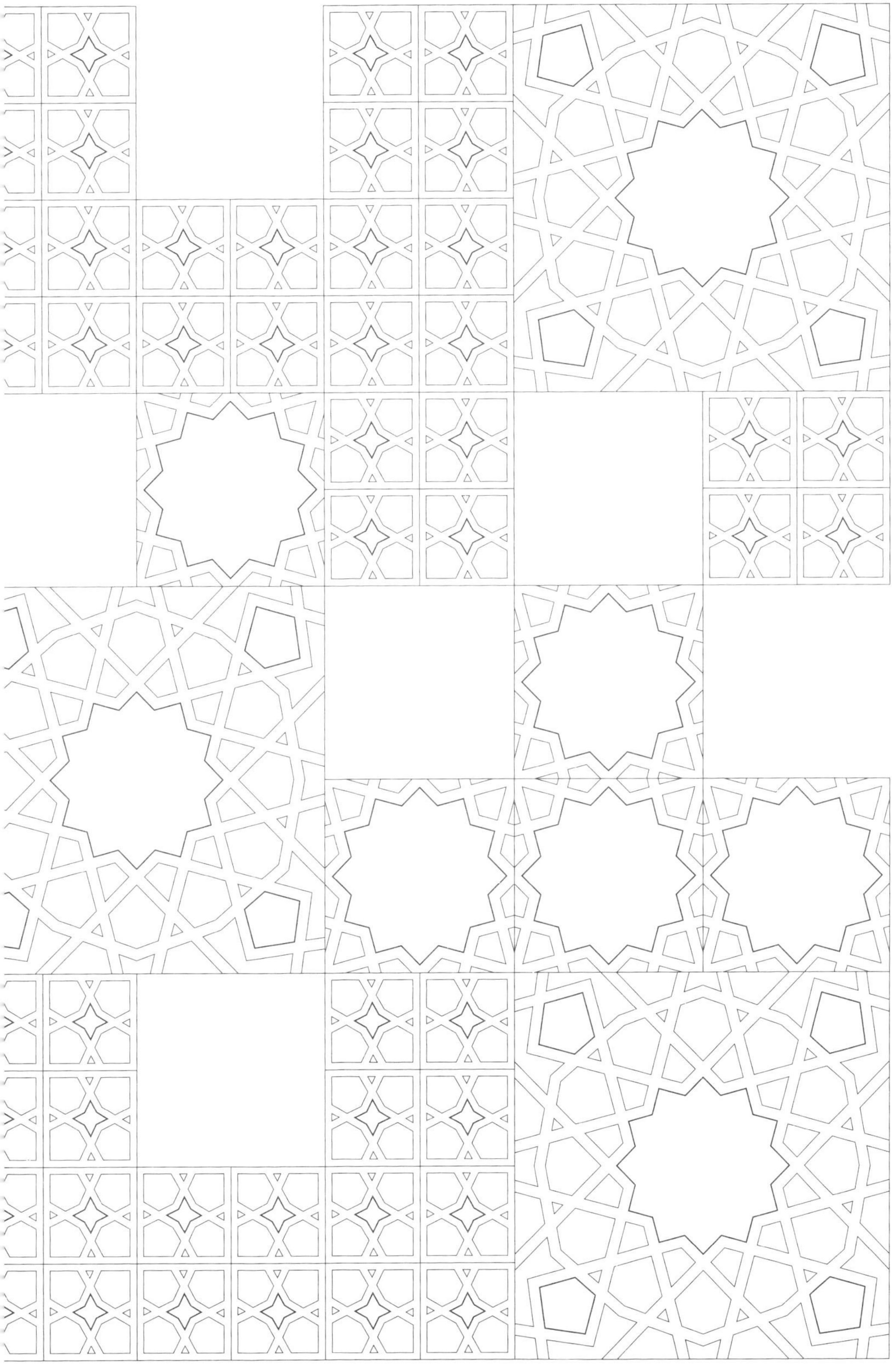

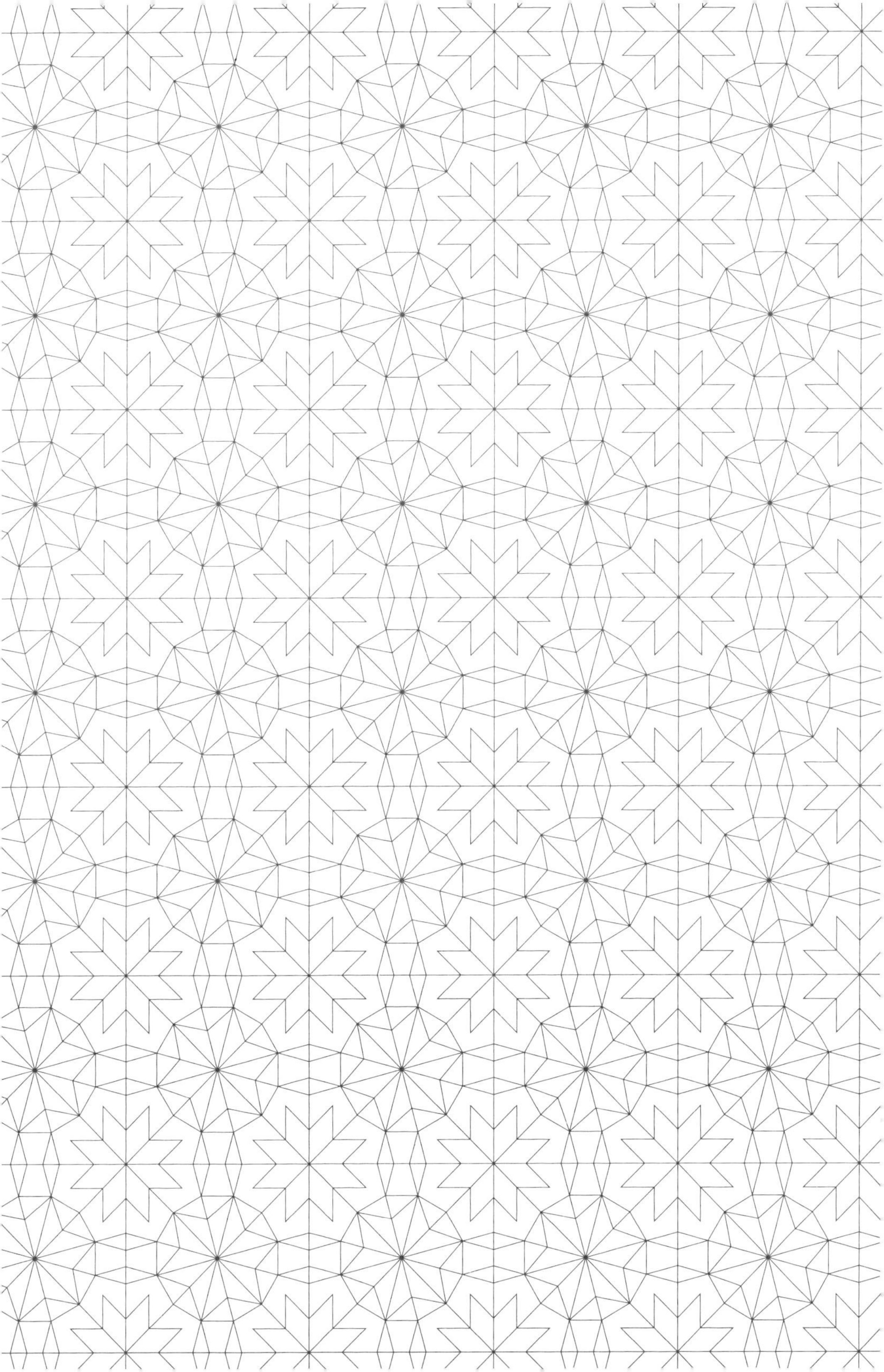

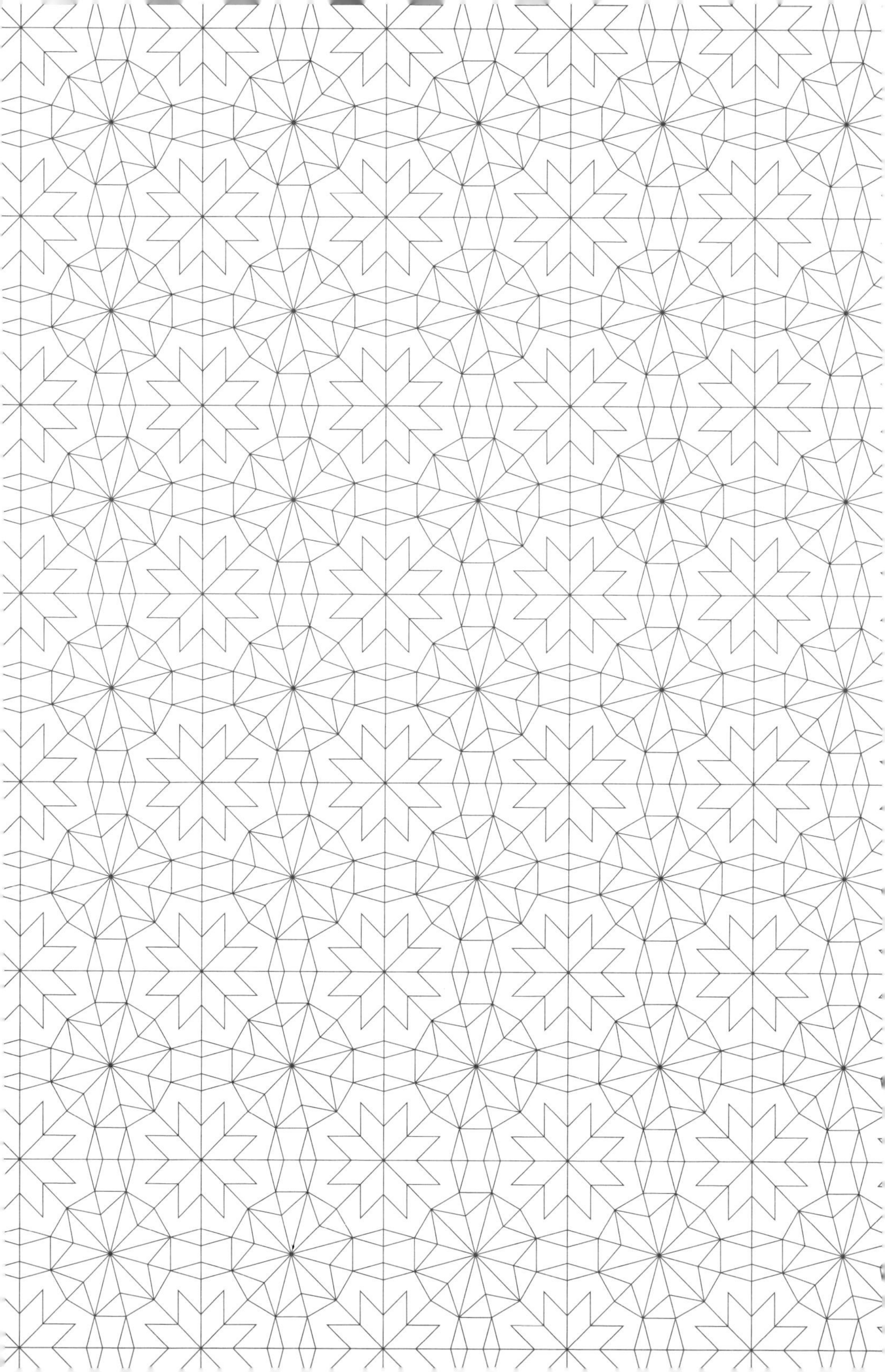

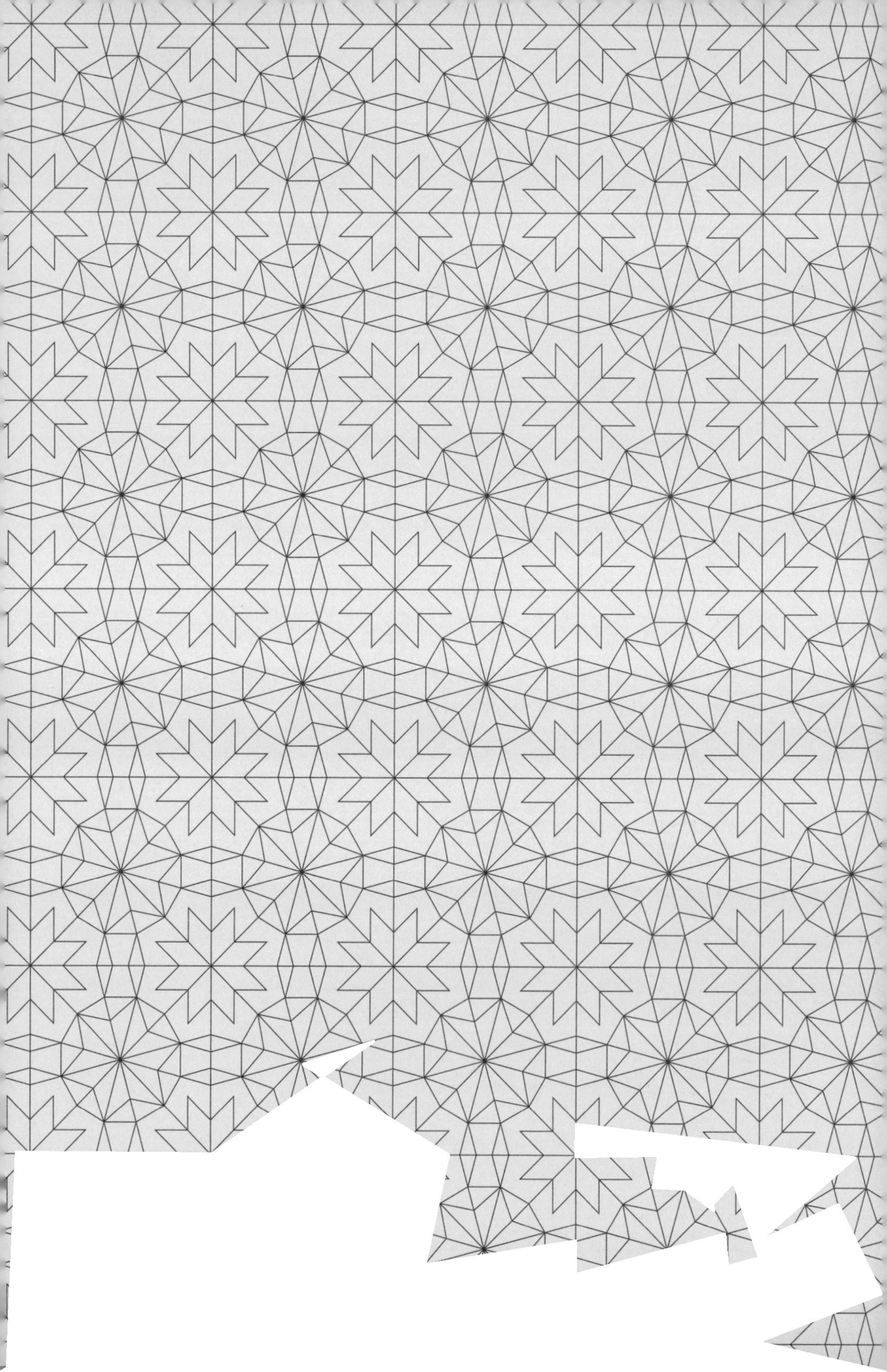

Dreamday Pattern Journal • Marrakech – Moroccan Style
© Laurence King Publishing | www.laurenceking.com | ISBN 978 1 78067 892 4 | Printed in China